DON BROWN

A Wizard from the Start

The Incredible Boyhood & Amazing Inventions of

THOMAS EDISON

HOUGHTON MIFFLIN BOOKS FOR CHILDREN
Houghton Mifflin Harcourt Boston New York 2010

For the Hill Family

All rights reserved. For information about permission to reproduce selections from
this book, write to Permissions, Houghton Mifflin Harcourt Publishing Company,
215 Park Avenue South, New York, New York 10003.

Houghton Mifflin Books for Children is an imprint
of Houghton Mifflin Harcourt Publishing Company.

www.hmhbooks.com

The text of this book is set in Minister Light.
The illustrations are a combination of digital imagery and watercolor on paper.
Book design by Carol Goldenberg

Library of Congress Cataloging-in-Publication Data is on file.

ISBN 978-0-547-19487-5

Printed in Singapore
TWP 10 9 8 7 6 5 4 3 2 1
4500202658

W<small>HAT CAN YOU SEE</small> from a hundred feet up?

In 1855, eight-year-old Tom Edison needed only to climb the tower next to his Port Huron, Michigan, home for the answer. The tower was the bright idea of his father, Samuel, who charged the curious twenty-five cents for a bird's-eye view.

Edison's tower earned Samuel a bit of local fame, but it didn't make the family rich. Neither did Samuel's lumber business, or his grain or grocery businesses.

Young Tom pitched in and helped plant the family truck garden. At harvest, he and his father loaded a horse and wagon with vegetables and sold them from door to door.

Still, the Edisons barely had enough to send Tom to school.

But his school days ended anyway when Tom's mother got wind of a teacher's cruel explanation for Tom's classroom daydreaming:

"Addled," the teacher said—another way of calling Tom confused or stupid.

Tom said his mother was "the most enthusiastic champion a boy ever had. . . . [She] angrily told the teacher that he didn't know what he was talking about."

Afterward she schooled Tom herself at home.

"My mother taught me to read good books quickly and correctly, and . . . this opened up a great world of literature," Tom said.

He read history and philosophy books. He read books on mechanics, electricity, and chemistry. They inspired Tom to make a laboratory in the Edisons' cellar. With a pal, he experimented with acids and chemicals.

Poor Mrs. Edison worried that they would "blow [their] heads off."

At twelve, Tom became a railroad "news butch," and rode the train back and forth to Detroit, selling newspapers, magazines, candy, and cigars to the commuters. He worked fourteen hours a day, and his business grew.

But Tom still found time on the train for chemistry experiments in the baggage car. After one experiment started a fire, an angry railroad worker boxed Tom's ear.

Most days, waiting in Detroit for the return ride home, Tom visited the public library. He'd start at the first book on a bottom shelf and read one after another until it was time to move to the next shelf.

Clever Tom also scavenged discarded equipment from Detroit's newspaper's print shop and used it to write and print his own newspaper on the train, *The Herald*. He charged eight cents a month and had several hundred readers.

In one article, fourteen-year-old Edison wrote, "The more to do, the more to be done," a slogan the busy boy could have taken as a personal motto.

During this time, Tom began to notice that his hearing was fading. Had the angry railroad worker caused it? Or had it been the fault of the conductor who lifted Tom aboard a train by his ears? Was it the result of the scarlet fever he'd suffered earlier? Or something he inherited? No one can be entirely sure.

Along with his hearing, Tom's interest in his business also faded. He discovered it was much more fun hanging around telegraph offices.

There was no telephone yet, and the telegraph offered the fastest way to send messages. A telegraph operator used a "key" to tap "dots" and "dashes"—short and long clicks. Arranged in a certain order, the clicks stood for letters. Dot-dash was the letter *A*; dash-dash-dot-dot, the letter Z. Messages could be made of long strings of the correct clicks.

Mastering the key and making sense of the clicking messages were the hard-won skills of telegraph operators. People admired them for their smart, modern jobs, and Tom longed to be one. He haunted telegraph offices and collected bits of know-how.

While he was visiting one office near a railroad station, the three-year-old son of the telegraph operator wandered onto the track and into the path of a freight train.

Brave Tom dashed to the boy, scooped him up, and dove clear.

The grateful father rewarded Tom with telegraph lessons.

Studying eighteen hours a day, young Edison became a better operator than his teacher in just weeks, and he was soon hired at a small telegraph office in Port Huron.

"I was . . . industrious. . . . After working all day, I worked in the office nights as well . . . I seldom reached home until 11:30 at night," he later said.

Keen for better pay and more challenging work, sixteen-year-old Tom left sleepy Port Huron and became a tramp telegraph operator, traveling from one office to another.

The next six years found Tom in Indianapolis, Cincinnati, Louisville, Memphis, and New Orleans.

He became a terrific operator, but that wasn't enough for curious Tom. He spent his free time tinkering with the telegraph machines and experimenting with electricity. He kept feasting on books, one after another.

In 1868, he took a job in Boston, Massachusetts, a city of experimenters and inventors. Excited by what he saw, Tom tried his hand at it, and worked on printing telegraphs, fire alarms, and machines that could transmit pictures.

Finally, Edison quit his operator's post to devote all his time to his inventions.

At twenty-two years old, he invented an electric vote-recording machine to be used by state governments. For it he received his first patent, an official recognition that the machine was the invention of Thomas Alva Edison.

The machine was a flop. No one wanted it.

Vowing to never invent things that wouldn't sell, Tom decided to find out what the world needed, then "go ahead and invent it."

From his laboratory came improved telegraphs, a stock ticker, an electric storage battery, the phonograph, and motion picture cameras, to name just a few.

Then, in 1879, Thomas Edison invented the electric light bulb. No longer would flickering candles or the wicks of whale oil and gas lamps light the world by fire. Instead, the "little globe of sunshine" would brighten people's lives.

Clever Tom, energetic Tom, brave Tom, hard-working Tom, curious Tom transformed the world forever with his inventions. His vision proved more remarkable than the view from any tower—with it, he could see . . . the future.

Speaking of the 1,093 patents he earned in his life, Tom said, "I never did a day's work in my life. It was all fun."

Author's Note & Bibliography

THOMAS ALVA EDISON was born on February 11, 1847, in Milan, Ohio, but spent most of his childhood in Port Huron, Michigan. For much of this time, he was known as Al.

Edison credited his mother's homeschooling for his love of reading and books. His extensive reading made him a freethinker and led to his nontraditional notions of religion. He would later attest, "What [others] called God I call nature, the Supreme Intelligence that rules matter."

His 1,093 inventions spanned electric power, telecommunications, motion pictures, sound recordings, storage batteries, and cement production. They were the product of not only his fertile imagination but also his New Jersey laboratories in Menlo Park and West Orange, forerunners of the modern research and development facilities. Hundreds of companies bore his name; one of the most enduring is New York City's power company, Consolidated Edison.

(Still, an Illinois man bests Edison with 1,321 patents. But nearly all of the new champ's inventions relate to the florist business; no inventions on the order of the light bulb or phonograph there.)

Edison proved himself a ruthless business competitor. Pioneering motion picture producers resented his equipment monopoly. The rise of the movie capital Hollywood was due in part to its great distance from Edison and the enforcement of the inventor's patents.

Another epic business battle pitted Edison against Nikola Tesla, a former employee. Tesla's system of electrical power called alternating current, or AC, was an alternative to Edison's electrical system direct current, or DC. AC was superior for several reasons, including its ease in transmitting over long distances. But Edison countered that AC was more dangerous and could cause fatal electrocutions. To prove his point, he conducted public electrocutions of animals, including a circus elephant named Topsey. Modern viewing of Edison's film of the death of Topsey will give even the most ardent of Edison fans pause. Despite Edison's grotesque theatrics, Tesla's alternating current became the electrical standard.

Edison died in 1931.

Baldwin, Neil. *Edison: Inventing the Century.* New York: Hyperion, 1995.

Clark, Ronald W. *Edison: The Man Who Made the Future.* New York: G. P. Putnam, 1977.

Delano, Marfe Ferguson. *Inventing the Future.* Washington, D.C.: National Geographic Society, 2002.

Israel, Paul. *Edison: A Life of Invention.* New York: John Wiley & Sons, 1998.